C000120805

The Mouth of Eulalie

First published in 2022 by Blue Diode Press
30 Lochend Road
Leith
Edinburgh EH6 8BS
www.bluediode.co.uk

All rights reserved. No part of this book may be reproduced, stored in a retrieval system, or transmitted in any form, or by any means, electronic, mechanical, photocopying, recording or otherwise, without prior written permission from Blue Diode Press.

Poems copyright © Annie Brechin, 2022.

The right of Annie Brechin to be identified as author of this work has been asserted in accordance with Section 77 of the Copyright, Designs and Patents Act 1988.

ISBN: 978-1-915108-01-2

Typesetting: Rob A. Mackenzie.
text in Minion Pro.

Cover photograph: © aliisik, Shutterstock.
Back cover image: © natalypaint, Adobe Stock.
Cover design and typography: © Rob A. Mackenzie.

Diode logo design: Sam and Ian Alexander.

Printed and bound by Imprint Digital, Exeter, UK.
https://digital.imprint.co.uk

The Mouth of Eulalie

Annie Brechin

Blue Diode Press
Edinburgh

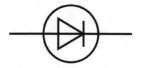

❧

"Think you there was, or might be, such a man
As this I dreamt of?"
— *Antony and Cleopatra, Act V Scene II*

❧

Contents

London, 2008

1. The Mouth Of Eulalie

This cotton has wrapped me for three days.
Your semen glues and then flakes.

Shall I pretend I sat in the study
reading the lives of saints?

The laundry goes round in the machine.
Would a list of dates be safe?

Would you like a cup of coffee. Sex.
It is eternally contingent.

We are alone in our dream.
How does intentionality form?

Your plane will land.
I'll wear my prettiest summer dress.

And I'll tell you the story:
young girl, hard times.

A man of power tortured her.
After they tore at her sides

with metal hooks, they set her on fire.
Inflamed her.

Poor snow-muffled dawn.
Implosion of feathers.

The warmth, yes.
The trembling softness.

Pull the sticky, shiny panties out.
Emerging beatified.

Next time you say
you'll take me with you.

I imagine a picnic ruined
on the wide empty grass.

My love, let me put
your cock into my mouth.

It will sound like
I know what I'm doing.

2. Sex Threatens Equilibrium

Listen. We slept together.
It was a mistake.

Four times. Four mistakes?
Or the same mistake?

Like the poor suicide
always trying to kill the same self.

Mis-take. As if reaching for one thing
the hand returned another.

I told him once he was bad in bed.
Bad or wrong? Bad for me.

All we really know is
she was engaged in something.

Eventually there was the ring
a large square cut emerald.

3. Only That We Love

The Tate. It's the civilised
thing to do.

Sleep brings itself
it is the only name of the goddess.

Or do we call it to us?
Dreams, the excreta –

But so are memories, held
to be released over and over.

How many times have I seen
that flush mount to your cheekbones?

It all builds to a picture:
this is what he looks like when he comes.

Inconsolable marble, I said
of *The Kiss*.

But why should marble wish
to be consoled?

We do not know the lover
only that we love.

4. How Others Perceive Us Is Not How We Perceive Ourselves

Juliette, pinned to the twisted sheets.
Juliette, frantic as an emerald.

Certainly you saw a body.
The first thing that you saw.

How constantly we check our image!
Screens, tv, laptop.

Our own personal cult of celebrity.
So evident we forget

it's an accumulation of images.
Juliette, frantic as an emerald.

And the woman
who could use language like a sword

reduced to a body on its back.
Legs agape.

5. The Truth Value Of Art Is Based On Recognition

My name is Juliette Larson.
She tries saying things into the mirror

to see if there is any recognition.
I am twenty-five years old.

I love my husband.
And I doubt the truth of art.

We suspend our disbelief
to enter into another world.

Even if I could know you
I would never know if I should believe you.

6. Personal States Are Private

It's comforting to hold
food in the mouth.

Oral fixation.
The psychosexual horoscope.

I've given up smoking
but I used to smoke.

Old Eliot on his boiled sweet.
Straws? Alcoholism.

Not without the walls of my pride.
If the walls were not there

I would be needy.
I am needy,

but not outside the walls.
A different meaning.

Fortresses fall
in the space between our definitions.

You might as well hold
the words back in your mouth.

7. Emotion Is The Lens Through Which Everything Is Focused

We are not looking at the same tree.
We are not looking the same at the tree.

But it's the same tree we see everyday.
Time is a stream

but existence is a point
(I can see my house from here).

Let's wait for something here.
For a lie needs to be told.

The same is not true of the truth.
Either our perceptions are true or false

Or they are the state of affairs.
Contingent on their content.

I could be in love with anyone.
It needn't even be love.

And yet it must!
Words must be used.

But love is not an apple.
I wish to define – intentionality.

What is sanity?
Separate out love.

I could drown in my love.
Why this particular death

whose characteristic is to overwhelm?
Love is the state of affairs

and when it is lost
I will be negated in this state.

8. Each Exchange Is A Competition

I want to give the audience a leg-up.
Shall we attempt a normal view?

Clockwork of a weekday.
Gym at eight, office at nine.

Coffee cups and lipsticked up.
Sometimes an hour

before Facebook.
This generation keeps in touch.

There is no depth to boredom
it is a thin line you follow indefinitely

which is the outline of the word
written in pale grey ink.

The parts of my day which I live separate
do not leave me gasping for your presence.

It is because here you are a dream
that is always with me.

Keep checking the phone for texts.
I remember the first time

you asked me for a photo.
It was a while before I got it right.

Do you want my face or only my flesh.
The genitals blind with need.

There are a hundred on file now.
None of them look like us.

Evenings are a round of cocktails and dinner parties.
Your hand on the back of my neck.

Sometimes I think you want me
so people can see you get what you want.

Strangely I feel less like a trophy
when you dress me.

The short black skirt. Yes
yes, the stockings.

9. We Can't Trust The People That We Love

The laundry is folded in a drawer with lavender.
Housework gives a feeling of associated purity

like raping an angel.
One day I was on my hands and knees

scrubbing away.
I was in a loose summer dress.

Ah he says. The French maid scenario.
Sex is only sex before it's itself.

Then it's this thing.
His every fingerprint.

Unlike boredom there are depths to pleasure.
It is intimate, it's private.

What is dirty about accounts of sex
is their incompleteness.

If you love you can be trusted.
But we should not trust the ones we love.

Human beings are distinguished from animals
in that we fuck face to face.

Now answer me
is this bravery or cowardice?

10. Synesthesiac

On Thursday the rain unexpectedly
through warm air.

Naked shoulders and a plate
of bread and butter.

Amber purple.
Came harder, then it ebbed and blew.

I went in through the balcony door,
was come in

to sit on the bed and listen
for that clean earthy smell.

I am not questioning if you exist.
You exist and are unknowable.

11. Adoration = Weakness

I flake old friends
like a tree flakes bark.

We used to be the blood of one another
I have new blood.

They are old bones.
Crackle in your coffins of platitudes.

Characters are endlessly opaque.
What is Juliette?

All she aspired to be.
Secure, adored.

A man's woman.
She is powder and paint.

She disappears regularly into the toilets
to restate her face.

The problem is not that I want you
more than I ever thought possible to want a man.

The problem is I want you exactly the way
I always thought possible to want a man.

12. If We Are Not Whole Can We Repeat/Intend?

Occam's razor is too sharp
for everyday use

unless one employs a mirror.
Balance is my god.

Something is taken for granted, taken
in the assumption it will be given.

With your clear arms in the moonlight
one night you told me you were lonely.

I sleep get up walk fragmentary lie down
wrap myself in your absence.

Allergies to the dust mites in the carpet
allergies to the god of war.

Little broken bits of sky
little broken bolts of silk.

Sun: white in the morning
rose gold when it's waning.

Moon: dove grey
beaten by the gong of the lit lamp.

The dome the gong of the lit lamp.
It is a very heavy presence.

Switch down and the moon back
flying between the curtains which are

blue like your favourite colour and not
the colour of my eyes.

Why do I see you as a figure of conflict?
From you emanates my strongest suspicion of the Other.

Because you transcend my view.
You have isolated me.

To love the unknown exposes you to a risk:
incompleteness in your own being.

Simple conclusion yet
look at the consequences.

He makes her think
there is something wrong with her.

For the self must be complete
to repeat coherently.

But she's tied to him now. Her husband.
Stink of masochism.

Faint tremblings in the water of the marriage
faint element of distress.

Why the fuck are we even discussing this shit?
Something has started to smell like shark-bait.

Agonies of an off-white dress.
Agonies of champagne and cool pews.

Agonies of yellow roses.
Above the tied cravat the space between neck and ear.

All the sideways glance could take in
facing the priest I I yes I do yes I I I.

Anything to be able to touch the space behind the jaw
with the tip of my tongue.

Therefore the day did not shatter.
Therefore I flew out of myself.

We break up the scene into things
so we can attach certain attributes to them

so that we can make predictions.
For if we cannot predict, how can we intend?

13. This Darwinist Pap

Yes I know there was another
in the beginning.

Well as for me I was fucking my boss
like a good little corporate whore.

You used to make me talk about our encounters
as you bent me over the kitchen sink.

Did he finger you in the lift?
Were you even wearing panties?

If I hadn't fucked him that day
I used to make something up.

I met yours later, out with some friends.
It was a little while after the wedding.

She told me how you'd spent Christmas together
that December I stormed off to Scotland.

It lasted until New Year's Eve. Drunk in the snow
you breathed steam on a window

and wrote I [heart] then my name.
Then I knew you talked.

Four times a mistake. Fine.
I carry on fucking the boss.

Not that we stopped.
But it was a hellish kind of limbo.

My flat leaked everything leaked. Water
streamed down the light bulb, the smoke detector.

I phoned my friend Marie.
You were there (at 2 am?).

What's happened?
Fucking ceiling's falling in.

You know they used to dunk mad people
in water to try to purge them.

I've read my Foucault.
We were never this elegiac in speech.

I would like to think of us as movie stars
perfectly scripted.

Someone is fucking with the timeline
let's call it memory.

Thread it on a string
like your dirty laundry.

When were you still seeing the nameless girl?
When did I see her, drunk on the street?

To think I believed you loved me
because a nameless girl told me so.

14. Historically, Men Control Women's Sexuality

But what do you really want?
said the boss.

We were having coffee.
Our parents drank tea.

I want only to want him
and know a child is sleeping down the hall.

Domesticity, no!
You're a Bad Girl.

Did you marry the whore?
What did you take to the altar?

All the times with your cock in my ass.
Your semen drooling down my leg that morning.

Not supposed to see the bride before the wedding.
In the ensuite hiding from the bridesmaids.

Back then
I was not even Juliette Larson.

15. The Questioning Of Love Is Internal

I wrote to you from Scotland:
Whole hours go by and I do not think of you.

Went hiking up the tor
with my brother and sister.

Raincoats spread out like wings.
Always the sea lapping at the edge of hearing.

When I love you do I love god?
No it's filthier than that.

Like being strangled with pondweed.
Green sludge tugging at the oesophagus.

Christmas is the same as every year.
We double our reflections.

The year before Gran died, that was bad.
She could barely remember who we were.

Her eyes scared and groping.
Like a beaten child, please be kind?

All these letters I burnt.
Then I came back down here to see you.

16. Photos Do Not Constitute A Real Interaction

The longer you are gone
the further everything recedes.

The sun dying over the rooftops
the faithful sun strong and orange at the end of it all.

Taking the lamb out of the marinade
placing it on the roasting tin

the scent of rosemary strong and rising.
As perfume rises from the throat.

I try to remember the way your teeth met in my neck.
How wet it made me.

I try looking at your photos
to see if they remember you.

It could be another
grinning photoshopped beside me.

If we are all individuals
what is the one, what is the I.

This immense and limitless void
behind my eyes, the sum of all knowledge

the bound creature of immediate experience.
For the mind is not an empty box.

17. Human Being Always Searching For Patterns

Office hours off we go
into the grey.

Sit around growing soft and white
like cotton-wool bread.

The management are away.
We go out for a long lunch

and come back drunk.
Girls swap makeup stories in the toilet

boys boot round a basketball.
Sweepstake on the Grand National.

Someone rings out for pizza.
Kids without a teacher.

Spam comes daily through the filter
like a horoscope. I treat it as such.

I signed up to French conversation
and did not wear my silk nightdresses for a month.

The Swiss one
decided the location of our skiing holiday.

I deliberately left a hammer in plain view
but nobody commented.

You're getting married
isn't that what you wanted?

When I got home, the living room was already vacant.
Mais tu es un vrai philosophe.

He pulled her down so that they were kneeling face to face.
With you I'm not afraid I'll be satisfied.

Pit your skills against me one more time.
Returns the size of the rope. Battle noises, sounds of sword
    striking.

Concentrate that you should have had to suffer.
His very name was likely a death sentence.

It was so sweet to believe this amused abandonment
was meant for me.

18. It's A Marriage. We're Supposed To Belong To Each Other

Are you ordering new business cards?
You're ordering them with his name on, right?

Secretaries. They love that shit.
If they're married, they talk about their own wedding.

If they're not, they're either planning it
or they love the vicarious thrill.

If they're divorced
then you get the warnings and advice.

What else have we been talking about for months?
(The recession: the company will go down the pan.)

I think you're doing this
to prove you belong to him.

19. Like God I Can See The Present

Sweetness – yes, there is sweetness.
Some mornings are lavender.

Like the word rain-washed.
Munching on a raisin bagel I offer you some

you say no thanks. Then,
I can still taste you.

The gym pumps me up
my colleagues are funny

clients polite with problems
complex yet solvable.

I have no problem calling you mine.
We are given by the rings we wear.

It is sweet to be married.
Everything we want will come to us in time.

Not because I can see the future but like god
I can see the present

and I see us for what we are
those who will obtain all they want.

20. Recognition Of Form Is Crucial

Sundays spent on the sofa
watching old movies.

Argument, playful cushion in the gut.
We get up, fuck…

The formula is comforting
we know its confines.

Fluffy cowboy land.
Like toddlers taking steps.

But allow art is adolescence
admired at all points

where it subverts the archetype.
Recognition of the form is central.

21. Isn't It A Wife's Right To Know Her Husband Loves Her

Arguments. Plates slammed against the wall.
You think I give a fuck what you think.

Shatter shatter little crisp notes
like someone stepping on cellophane.

If only it was the evening
and not the middle of the day.

But you can't ask an Englishman
to take his wife to bed at noon.

We'll settle this later.
Got to go back to work now.

Mouth opens like a tulip.
What is the form of a marriage?

22. The First Audience Is The Artist

I know he loves me because he cooks me
poached egg on toast every morning.

Sometimes with those tiny Italian fungi from the market.
Sometimes a smoky Dutch cheese.

Other people's standards.
Artaud would have understood that.

Civilisation was destroying
the spirit-in-the-flesh.

But these things can only be opposed personally.
Actors are the primary audience to the work

through their reaction they create
a second work, a transitory phantom

to which the audience participate
as if they were looking at a solid picture on a wall

but looking it at behind
a projected image of that picture.

Artaud wanted to make his audience actors.
The first audience remains the artist.

Artaud did not want to be enslaved
to logical thought.

Deleuze thought of thought (ha)
as rupture.

23. Each Encounter Is A New Engagement Resulting In New Work

The memory of spoken speech
is not the speech that was spoken

and each recollection is a new speaking.
The work is constantly collaborative

as much with the last audience
as with the first.

For what is the value of words?
A frame allows thingness.

But you must engage with the painting yourself.
There is a frame with your name on it.

I don't know where to hang it.
It contains the entire world.

What is more endless and yearning
than the struggle of a dissociated mind for unity.

I am not sure
I believe in the Oriental mind of unity.

Can you not shut up about Artaud for five minutes?
I'm trying to watch the Grand Prix.

Instead of the I Ching
I use the fragments of Sappho.

In fact lies need to be told, transitive.
Juliette cannot tell when he is lying or not.

We break ourselves down.
Somehow in going to you

I left myself behind.
And ever since have felt guilty.

But Sappho also said: Foolish woman!
Have no pride about a ring.

24. If You Can Entertain, You Can Control

A new production of Lorca's *The Public*.
One of our friends was in make-up.

She got to paint this gorgeous Iranian actor
red for the crucifixion scene.

She let him do his own bollocks.
The play doesn't ask questions

it provides a scenario then
you ask yourself questions.

Were you shocked?
How do you know Jesus wore a loincloth?

For hundreds of years
people's first contact with drama was through religion.

Away in the night
sound of a silk dress ripping.

Not even making it upstairs
into the utility rooms for candles.

25. Duende

We have not soul but duende
the passion of the soul

passion which means also martyrdom
emotion taking power from death.

A passionate soul would own its own death
and be a ceaseless expression of it.

26. We Are Unconsciously Withheld From Others

In my dream you, the non-smoker,
are smoking a cigarette.

We are sitting at the edge of a large field
extending out into darkness.

A few of us are here but not many
we are all close friends.

Although I cannot see their faces and I know
if I looked I would not recognise them.

'We' sounds wrong.
I am not the owner of the dream

simply one of those watching you
watching as you talk.

You wave your hands and I know
the exact instant you have forgotten the cigarette.

I look in your eyes in that moment
the moment when the cigarette is part of your hand

as much as finger and bone and I know
something is being withheld.

You do not mean to withhold it
but if I asked you for it, you could not give it to me.

27. Men Fear Female Desire

Hotels are the same everywhere.
What's the point

if you're not going to leave the room?
Might as well be your own room.

One of his family's interests:
a vineyard in the Languedoc.

Hills raked to red gutters
the white villa on the edge.

Morning walk to the bakery
golden crusts trembling in brown paper.

This lasts for three days
then Juliette gets thrush.

He takes refuge by taking control.
Darling, it happens to everyone.

Packs her full of live yogurt
drives her to the pharmacy

helps her stumbling tongue
la mycose

Then the pharmacist pronounces
No sex for a week, hein. Vous comprenez?

On their honeymoon.
So then what:

Endless markets in tiny interlinked shaded squares.
Enormous ripe tomatoes, transculent endives

solid racks of lamb. Slick white monkfish tails
long batons of baguettes

huge bulbs of garlic purpled
goats cheese moulded to black

and black bitter olives. In Lodeve
they gave out tiny espresso cups of wine

while you were waiting for your cheese.
Crumbling patisseries, palmiers swamping your hands.

How darkness falls in summer
like a welcome friend joining you at dinner

to share slabs of foie gras
exquisite rare steaks.

Drove down to the Etang
sat under striped awnings

drank divine white Picpoul
sampled oysters swamped with garlic.

Tiny tielle Setoise, soft pastries
of spiced octopus.

Lasted another five days still
less than a week.

Terrible the pressure between two sets of eyes
no diver could withstand.

Do you think it's ok?
Oh come on let's.

Although it would be nice
to have a little lubricant.

He rushes to the kitchen
comes back with virgin olive oil

then it is not just functional but beautiful.
Viscous and slipping everywhere.

Our skins are Greek gods and lotus stamens.
Heavenly globes were not more golden than her breasts then.

Now if only we had a maid
she could deal with the sheets.

Laughing into the shower.
Turn on the heat he yelps.

Twists to get the mirror on his back.
God. Is that blood?

I thought that only happened in movies.
Both shocked and wondering

did we do this?
Gaze slips suddenly to her nails.

No, but you did.
She is scared of what she has done.

He is scared that he is scared of her.
What to do. From this panic.

Gets back into the shower.
Let's do it again.

28. Acknowledge The Pain You Have Suffered

You smile at me, I smile at you
the heart lifts. But only so far.

Is that all there's meant to be then?
This fierce contentment.

To know the nature of the soul –
that it is a sword –

and that it is better
not to wield it?

We are not afraid of the dark now.
Whatever comes at you will be solid.

We must not allow ourselves
the masquerade of a cure.

Love is a dark thing
she thinks to herself.

29. Marriage Is Based On Endeavour

Save me, save me
from financial insecurity.

But did he really?
Did he really do that?

It's still his money.
The yellow satin morning

cold tiles of the kitchen floor.
Oh but I work.

Enough for the wide rooms of your home?
The tall curtains sweeping the floor?

What if he leaves me my god
the balcony.

The expensive holidays
the broad beaches of Morocco.

Do not leave me.
For the sake of the dye vats of Marrakech.

Is this all your love is
you little bitch?

Why marriage? Why not just live together
and be in love? Oh fuck off

with your hippy Birkenstocks.
We must struggle together.

We must be partners in some undertaking.
This undertaking must mean nothing

to anyone apart from ourselves
and we must be the only ones undertaking it.

Of course it is a test.
But to risk falling out of love in a marriage

the very concept of a marriage being
an estate of love –

30. Can A Capitalist Economy Have A Socialist Conscience

Here comes the wind again
making the door swing and bang

disarranging the sunbeams.
It is sweet to want for nothing.

An important part of me is missing
but I am quite happy about that.

If it comes back it will come secretly
like a fish slipping up a river.

Made Waterloo and you came clear
a salmon leaping upstream.

There is one who is not a passenger
but my love.

How is it that you move
when you are frozen as an image.

How your mouth tilts when you smile
that is another secret.

There is disquiet growing in me.
The tides of humanity.

I make you an island.
I set us both apart.

But then how can we live conscientiously?
Have honour.

How can I love you
if I am not honourable?

I don't know where to start!
What does one do.

Give to charity
become a doctor.

Call centres, useless jobs…
Just because you don't tear crops

from the earth with your bare hands
doesn't mean you are useless.

Can you honestly believe in the state?
Somewhere in your argument is the stink of pride.

Want to be a saviour
I yes I I can heal you.

Some people never make it big.
You're assessing their needs based on your own.

Come back to bed, Juliette.
Come back to my bent head.

The wind is calling my name again
the airplanes are sighing it

they are bright blades in the sky.
My lover is in my head my beloved.

Through fields of corn come to me.
Through the girders of the city.

An important part of me is missing
and when you return

it will have vanished
as if it never existed.

31. Social Conscience Vs Art Vs Ego

Will you love me forever?
When I think D&G stands for Dolce and Gabbana

not Deleuze and Guattari?
When I break my leg

and can't ski and you meet
some Nordic blonde on the slopes.

It took me so long to find you
I almost couldn't bear it when I did.

Almost couldn't forgive you
exactly because it had taken so long.

Couldn't forgive the nights of loneliness
and those men eating pieces of my heart.

I waited a long time to be your wife.
I remember wandering the streets of London.

Sometimes the body was full
sometimes it was silent.

Sometimes I was drunk
sometimes there was vomit.

My hands were cold inside my gloves.
There were Sunday afternoons in November

when the slate grey sky rained slate grey
over slate grey rooves

and all there was to do
was lie on the sofa and masturbate.

My friends were blind
to the intricacy of one another's careers.

I must get out of here.
And daily being faced with my own cowardice.

Wanted to be a saviour.
Well not me.

Safe behind a desk
banging the boss.

Then you come along and
we all know she played her cards right with that one.

Looked into your eyes
down at my hand only aces.

Too late I realised
we were playing with different decks.

Daily being faced with my own cowardice
the reaction is to seek revenge.

On the self or the world?
Vengeance is a mirror.

32. The Abortion Dress

Orange-red like a poppy
faded just a little from the sun.

Silk and striped
finishing at mid-thigh.

I had worn the Abortion Dress all summer
with my beige linen blazer

worn it loafing around markets
tip-tapping into little bistros

strutted in its briefness
it was not a dress now but an accomplice.

Importantly it was not the type of dress
one would wear to an abortion.

I waited. My legs were beautiful
in long black ribbed socks.

I watched husbands and birth control posters
with the same blunted curiosity.

In the next room there were only women.
The herd by the abattoir.

Someone offered me a guidebook of Iceland.
I forgot most of it, maybe it was the drugs.

The nurse offered me a laundry basket.
For your dress.

Ok, you want to keep it on?
Fine. Just your knickers then.

It was a small pleasant room
yellow like a breakfast room.

The doctor, pleasant
to the point of exuberance.

Entirely unthreatening.
I don't remember leaving the room.

After an hour of sipping water
I went and threw up.

Came back had a cup of tea.
A Spanish girl was telling another first timer

not to worry. You feel queasy
at first then it's ok.

I felt included in her kindness.
All the time I had been worried

I would be late to meet my parents' train.
We took them to that Argentinean place

such fantastic steaks.
Ten days later

tired of my 'heavy period'
I let you fuck me on the wooden floor.

The floor was hard
somehow we rolled off the rug

and my back was hurting.
I didn't mind though because

you made me come.
You were always very good at that.

33. South Bank Time

He is moving so quickly he almost
doesn't hear me.

Then the sound catches up to his ear
jogs over, *Sorry I'm late*

the train you know...
It's ok, you're on South Bank time.

South Bank on a bank holiday in May
the air like a cotton cardigan.

Long wooden benches outside the NFT
tables and tables of secondhand books.

Satsuma bindings of old Penguins.
Finger the worn soft cover

like you would stroke a cat's belly.
It's ready to be spring.

Let's go and get a drink. Fruit beer.
I saw some burgers back there.

Three oysters and a glass of wine
for a fiver. Don't think I'd trust that wine.

Look at these mushrooms.
Chinese medicine, yeah.

Gives you the memory of a lion.
Androcles, the Greek slave.

Daniel in the lion's den.
(This from the stallkeeper.)

Uh, I guess I'll go with a mushroom sandwich then.
Days like this guess at perfection

but wisely avoid it.
They seem so rare among the clutter

of laptop and privilege.
We are broken into by sunlight.

34. Absence Is Fictive

The seashell of the stairs.
The bathroom light is on.

It throws me like –
maybe you are home already?

Skimmed in quickly
you will wander now into the kitchen

sleeves rolled up
smelling of cricket lawns

like you do every weekend.
With all that beautiful slow energy.

We should go to the Tate more often, babe.
Down to South Bank.

How's dinner going?
I turn the light off.

Through the bathroom window
I can see the crescent of the new moon

a fingernail print in the skin of the sky.
Letting the pure light through like blood.

35. We Are Spoiled By Pleasure

How do you get me to do
the things you do, right from the start?

Sucking my panties clean
after you wipe the come from between my legs.

Is it the way you bury your teeth
in my shoulder?

You hardly speak about sex.
Right up until the point

when you push me against the wall I think
you're never going to touch me again.

When you do touch me I'll do anything
because it might be the last time.

I can almost forget I'm there until
you whisper, you're beautiful.

I used to hate that until I realised
this is the one time that beauty is of use.

Oh when will you get home?
It is expected pleasures that damage us.

Poor fool mooncalf
stuffing my thoughts with you

greedy with remembering you
vomiting your faults, your failings

spewing over your icon
only in an excuse to redeem you

set you up again on that pedestal.
I could have been in the park

in the sunshine with friends
reading a book, watching a movie.

How disgusted I am with myself
for gorging on you.

The horror of the beautiful summer day
is that it might never end

you might have to be this happy forever.
Promise you'll take me dancing.

Put your hands on my ass
kiss me a little drunk, a little sloppy.

You give me everything except
that you transcend my view.

But I want you to be unknowable
so I can spend a lifetime trying to know you.

36. Our Society Prizes Ambition Over Happiness

I was always good at my job.
Stopped screwing the sales guys

and saw them as objects in a process
I needed to maximise to achieve my goals.

The relationship between desire
and the outcome of desire

is not only dependant
but flows both ways.

37. We Must Be Responsible For Our Lives In Order To Enact Change

Are we responsible for our emotions?
How many hours did we argue this.

Decisions, control, back and forth.
It comes to something when you can't take responsibility

for your own body.
Are we responsible simply for arguing?

38. We Enter The World Through Our Bodies

Been lost since I saw a tree in a park
and it refused to become a word.

Stood shaking before it what was I
to it but the whole of everything.

Went home took off all my clothes
put on all my jewellery.

Bangles bracelets necklaces rings
toe-rings huge ropes of beads.

Then in front of the mirror
slowly stripped it off piece by piece

to see how autumn would feel.
Felt good but I didn't feel like a person any more.

Words are a split, a division.
Words are a form of memory.

Time is relative to consciousness
but constant to memory.

So we can conceive of the infinite
we just can't remember it.

The body doesn't know it's mortal.
It doesn't know it can stop.

It is our world and allows us to enter the world
and is and is enough.

39. Good Art Asserts Morality In Order To Be Valuable

If gnosis is kinesis
what is knowledge of art?

To encounter it not as perceptual object
but movement and transfer.

In good art there has to be death.
For the idea of worth

mortality has to be asserted.
What of the artists who drag us

in front of this truth over and over?
A failed artist is always a failure.

Now Juliette, any greysuited monkey
could pivot her excel – go macro baby!

So she is judged on who she is
not what she creates.

Everyone else in a shitty job
hates their shitty job too.

Suddenly she has comrades.
The artist has only talent.

40. Desire As Being Ultimately Possessed By Someone

I want you very badly.
She puts her fingers between her legs.

This is want. It is not need.
Gluttony.

She starts to move them gently.
Then less gently.

I want you in malls
and on the tops of buses.

Watching another girl's legs.
Watching a rabbit behind the daffodils.

It is not unceasing
but it is never-ending.

Buying shoes I see my face reflected
in the black patent it is not my face

but yours the shopgirl staring at me
as if I'm a lunatic

this blush getting bigger and bigger
in the middle of Selfridges

surrounded by hair-flipping colts
of Saint Tropezed schoolgirls

and fuschia-lipped Brazilian matrons
give me the damn shoes.

Almost worse than the want
is not being able to articulate it.

Kneeling on all fours while you are behind me
doing _____

all I can say is yes. Can't find the word
for what you do to me.

Would you want to see the want?
It's embarrassing I think.

Did you want me before you knew me?
She sighs gets up.

Pulls an oven glove over her wet hand.
Did you want to be in love?

Useless questions. The lamb
is placed tenderly before the knife.

41. Power Games

The first night you let me stay over
we toasted your compliance

with a ten-year-old Talisker
like honey and violet it was

velvet, violent.
The sex was better.

You drove me home at 6am
I showered and changed into work clothes.

The short skirt, the boots
the tuxedo jacket. And a man's tie.

Got into work on the dregs.
All day everyone came up to me

saying how chic I looked
was I going for an interview?

I got shit done.
I was shit hot.

Marie came over laughing, saying
it must have been a while.

Suddenly I felt awful
so entirely in your power.

What is fidelity but obedience?
When I show love it means chains.

Why am thinking like this!
This is not how I think when you're here.

Open the French windows.
The street below is full of people.

Soon he will walk steadily through the flow
he will be impatient on the stair.

His hurried step and his hand
through the wing of his hair.

42. How Long To Make Ourselves Acceptable To Thee

I have burnt my forehead on my hair.
That last sweep of the straighteners.

If only it was autumn and woodsmoke
could drift in to cover the smell.

In observance of these varying rituals
do I await the coming of my lord.

Cut the cuticles, file then enamel.
Their stupid names

Bubblicious or Goldspun Coral.
Their Mills and Boon chat.

So many of these rituals
you know little about.

Which cream is for the face and throat
which for the hands, the breast and body.

Which scent alights exactly where.
Now I take the file to the feet

it is less pretty. Now how long do we need
to make ourselves acceptable to thee?

Legs and pits plucked and greased.
Moustache any fifteen-year-old boy

would trade his stash of porn mags for
waxed off with a flourish.

Now tweezers tidy eyebrows.
Liner and pout, mascara.

One eye is unlined
her face Picasso'ed.

She needs to stop talking to the mirror.
Yes I could live without you.

But she leaves the letter unfinished
and goes to dress the salad.

43. Memory Can Be Wrong

There are notes on Lacan, never used.
There are entire cities abandoned by the gods.

Half my library is unopened.
Who first told me

make-up is used to simulate
what a woman looks like when she orgasms?

There are icicles on the air in Praguish Januaries
that are not more cold to the tip of my tongue

than the nape of your neck
as you turn away from me.

There was a man who when asked his name
lied charmingly, then gave me that lie

to be my own. And now I wear it above my brow
like a fake tiara.

Maybe I think too badly of you.
If we had a cat you would feed it.

You take the rubbish out.
You clear the path of leaves.

There is a lot to be said
for those who ease the way forward.

If I have remembered you wrong
I am sorry.

My body is the architecture of grief
but perhaps once it was filled with a loving choir.

Maybe the doors were open
and the hearth was tended.

I can smell the stone-baked bread
the oil and rosemary.

The wooden table is low.
The wine in an unlabelled casket.

It is that night again,
the night when he is with us.

The streets are expectant with cypresses
the light in the streets is like breath.

The faint lulling thrum
is the heartbeats of infants.

Sleeping. Breathing. Knowing
in complete ignorance that you will return.

44. Our Gods Are Smaller Yet Watch Them Proliferate

Marie's leaving Facebook.
She's what?

It's bizarre.
She's got this new boyfriend.

Doesn't he live in Salzburg?
Apparently they write letters.

I thought she was seeing someone before him
she's been acting strange recently.

He's ducked his head away
throat a long swallow of juice.

45. Why Is Love Unknowable

Did you really pick him up in Starbucks?
God, no. He picked me up in Starbucks.

The fatal embarrassment of forgetting her purse.
Then the deep voice behind her.

Of course he would pick up the lady's tab.
Like he does it every day.

It puts her back up.
She looks at him straight in the eyes

and there is something mischievous there.
She relaxes.

She's already thinking about him naked
and his weight over her.

What gives birth to love
is a quality that cannot be described.

The very being of another.
You can't know love, only feel it.

46. We Are Driven By The Fear Of Being Alone

'I charge ye, that if you find my beloved
that ye tell him that I am sick of love.'

Sick of love how?
Juliette hears this as a battle cry.

I am sick of love!
I am tired of it, I want no more.

I am sick of love!
Sick with it, pining and yearning.

She is deprived of her love-object.
Sick of being sick when she is without him.

If she left him what would she do?
How long would it take to find another.

She remembers for the millionth time
the look on Marie's face.

I'm sorry but we've got to let you go.
What kind of bullshit

management speak is that?
I'm really sorry.

Don't say that. You're supposed to be
my friend, my best friend.

It came from higher up.
Higher up, what is this? Nuremburg?

You're the only one on disciplinary.
You sly two-faced bitch.

No fucking vendetta Marie.
You were fucking up.

I don't want to be here telling you this.
But I've been telling you for months.

I fucked him you know.
Your precious husband.

He's screwed a lot of women.
Go pack up your desk, Marie.

After you were married.
I screwed him after you were married.

He came to my flat. Bored.
Restless. You know he gets that look –

I know he gets that look.
Just remember that

when you get home tonight.
Over my kitchen table.

47. Woman Are Taught To Have Unrealistic Expectations Of Marriage

I call him the Golden Man.
He inhabits the presence of many others.

Film stars, pop stars, the boys
who skinned knees with me in school.

Later – artists wounded in self-love
and my beloved herd of greysuits.

How could I expect a single man
to wipe him out?

48. Globalisation Leads To Unified Radical Factions

In Genesis, the Song of the Sword.
What is a sword but phallic?

It is not a sword that aspires to be phallic
but a penis wants to be sword-like.

So childlike we want these phalluses to protect us.
Babes in the wood, little Yankees.

Don't we envy their nuclear arsenal
their simply awful drawl

but mostly their soulful leader
who we could crown president of the world.

Juliette and her husband watch the Prague speech
his first public address in Europe.

Transfixed by his slight stammer
at the point of global collapse

finally there has appeared
this shining messianic figure.

A man of charm, intelligence
and it seems foresight.

They go about their sleepy Sunday
glazed in the dream of global government.

Well we've got to espouse something.
The era of sitting on our asses raking in profit

seems to have taken a nosedive.
Juliette was going to vote in the last general election

she was really. But
she had a hair appointment or something.

49. Organic Snobbery

I am living on Alpen bars
and the gentle mellifluence of the season.

I am glad you chose my best friend to fuck
we both share the same excellent taste in companions.

Nothing is more comforting
than the sound of you walking around downstairs

while I am up in the bedroom.
Are you making a cup of tea?

There is a cat who lives next door
a beautiful semi-Siamese

with a body the colour of warped toffee
and feet like chocolate dabs

she likes to sidle in through the casement
with the soft breeze and the white oleander.

You pause at the bottom of the stairs.
Will you come up to me? But no

you carry on to the study
balancing your book on your cup of tea

something virtuoso about markets.
Not the kind

where we pick out fresh fruit lazily on a Sunday.
I asked you about money.

Well are we safe enough?
It's all secure. Really.

I'm just supposed to take your word for it?
You never worried about it before.

You know how many redundancies we've had
in the last two months? More planned.

Anyone I know?
Here I could tell you.

Could reveal the depths of my ruthlessness.
They want me to sack Marie

and I'm going to do it.
Is it apathy or just pure fear

my neck will be next?
They the faceless they.

Sitting in a meeting with my boss
my erstwhile you-know-what

he looks drawn
drawn on, pencilled in

graphite marking the lines
deep and black.

He looks like a cartoon
all dragged out of shape

and I can't take my eyes off him.
Since Christmas it has been a nightmare.

First quarter results from a horror movie.
We need to reassess our resources.

Jesus, more? There's got to be something we can do.
My team hit target last month.

We only missed January.
The team hit. Not everyone in the team.

This is coming from the top.
How soon? As soon as possible.

We've put a package together.
Then you know who it's got to be?

50. Memory is not correct but transformative

How long have I been sleeping
a seed in the soil?

It is easier to sacrifice
self-respect than pleasure.

That long throat he would slit open
with a rugby shirt.

The function of memory is not to be correct
but to be transformative.

The function of memory is not to be correct
but to constitute the self

at a given time
based on the current situation.

51. If We Can Have Anything We Want, Does Anything Really Matter?

Do you want me to stop fucking you?
I want you never to have fucked her.

Well I can't give you what you want.
What the hell am I supposed to do then?

What do you do normally
when you can't get what you want.

I don't know. Can't remember
the last time I couldn't.

Little fingers of light dribbling down the skull.
That moment of terror.

Juliette is angry with herself
the ephemera of imagined conversations.

It is simple enough, decide
get on with it.

What if he lies?
If he says no I'll have no way to prove

he's not lying. If he says yes
we're screwed anyway

I'll have to leave him.
He wouldn't have respect for me

if I stayed.
For a moment

For every moment since she found out
she wonders what it would be like

to live without his scent and weight.
Her wall in the dark.

You'll have to ask him.
You could not.

Leaving him would be a little death.
Maybe the constant

visioning of his absence is the soul's way
of trying to encompass that death.

We are all being forced to face the fear of loss.
For the first time some of us.

Remember leaving uni, not worried
if we would get a job only

which job we would get.
I go to my boss.

I beg on my knees.
I want to beg on my knees but I don't.

I say *You can't fire her.*
She's my friend.

These are hard times.
Isn't there anything?

She is fucking my husband.
She is fucking my husband

and if we fire her
he might leave me.

Who the hell would say that?
I don't.

Yes you're right. You're right
of course we have to fire her.

I'm sorry I'll sort it out.
Get up, smooth the skirt.

Marie could have lied
she's done it before.

All relationships are polite fiction.
Juliette will never know the truth.

He found her in the dark kitchen
blue dark from the unopened blinds.

That great city out there, still moving
frantic in the far far distance.

She kept her back to him.
Come back to bed. It's four in the morning.

You're sick Juliette.
Take the day off work tomorrow.

What's wrong?
It is an unknowing in myself that cannot be known.

What if she'd said that
Said that to suit and cocktail parties

The gold watch and the villa in the south of France.
Whatever there is in me that is vital, I am losing it.

I want you to treat me like a princess
but I am not a princess.

52. Consumption = Goodness

This infidelity fear is boring.
Used to be afraid you didn't exist

used to be afraid
you didn't love me for me

not because there might be someone
you wanted more. How Heat magazine.

How trivial, how psychoanalytic
how lifestyle.

You never believe you will meet that person
who will turn your life upside down.

You are eager to meet them
but you believe you never will.

Then you do, and then suddenly
they are not there

and you are left hanging in your upside-down life
like a confused bat

tears running down your forehead.
You bend your body you drag it up.

Pull at whatever is there (don't look at it).
Pull until your nails break.

Bad news the Christmas lunch budget is cut.
The Rothschild secretaries will kill me

if they don't get their yearly chocolates.
Go negotiate with the boss then.

You do it, you're my team leader.
You need to work out how to sell it, Marie.

How can I love when I don't know
what love is, is the wrong question.

How can I love when I don't know
what the self is, you are getting closer.

Is it really believable that she would leave?
Given the dye vats of Marrakech

the grand bazaar of Istanbul
the vineyard on an Occitan incline.

Given she is unsure if she is woman or thing
the self or what is acted on, subject or object.

In her mind's eye she walks
and when she walks it is New York City

September 16th, it is Lehman Brothers
brown box time and nothing to be salvaged.

53. Sex Is The Only Form Of Physical Expression Left To Us

My heart has veins like the Westway at night
streams of wet light from tailbacks

of late commuters, ventricles with mirrored
frontages and facings of neon

intricate blood clots of cobbles
jumbled colours of shop and bar-fronts and the rain

and the unceasing and immeasurable movement of bodies
bodies which are vehicles no less than the taxis

disgorging businessmen and pleasure seekers into the same lit-black
    streets
hour after hour of the night into the grey morning

bleak from bridge to bridge, the air reverberating
with the silence between the cool canyons of glass and brick and steel.

But I remember harvest
the year when the walnut tree fruited for the first time

remember walking to the end of the garden
where it borders the hayfield with brambles

and stinging nettles and deep purple foxglove spears entwined
walking with bare toes in the damp grass

feeling the clay earth shift and give beneath
a delicious tension of resistance and acceptance

remember reaching the entire length of an arm upwards
a balletic movement

a movement almost, by this time, foreign entirely to this body
the body with elbows habitualised to the desk and keyboard

with rounded shoulders, with thought in its fingers not its frame
reaching and stroking the furred green spheres of the new fruit.

54. To Fail At Work Is To Fail At Living

If we position hope within our hearts
it makes it seem a nobler organ

not the meat fist that grinds us
daily onward without a yes or no from us.

The terror of exhaustion haunts me.
Living hand to mouth.

Stone pressing on the chest for eight hours
then the sword hanging above the head

all the bloodcrazy night.
The fear of unbecoming

that to fail at work
is to fail at life.

When we say work
do we mean art?

I have created spreadsheets
that would make Vermeer weep

vermillion streaks.
I can no more give up my work

than give over my own soul.
Is survival not a very war?

A battle on any ground –
worse, ground unchosen.

Aren't you proud of this war
proud of your strength

proud enough to risk it
marry a man you can't predict.

55. Infidelity = Independence

I do not believe in Tarot
in starscopes or the guts of birds

but sometimes you happen upon a certain line
in a certain book at a certain time.

'There'd be no surviving another winter here'
Cormac McCarthy, The Road.

Ruins of souls of strength and yearning.
I had thought that often and more often

before you interrupted me.
Thought it getting the train to Scotland

thought of not returning
an exquisite severance.

Of holding the soul to its own promises
to its lethal hopes of redemption.

Binding it with the ancient leathers of righteousness.
But you kept on interrupting.

First in the symbol of a word and then in its sound.
Then in the remembered body, the fierce and fire.

And how a bent arm would twist
against its own fragrant speckled blossoming.

Your hair under my hand
is like thick grass at summer. Verdant.

If you read your cards mythopoetically
the Lovers is the sun at its zenith.

Cold is pure and who wants purity?
Still if you examine the situation

there is a certain asceticism to my thoughts of you
even those strictly related to pleasure. Especially those.

Anything that strict must be ascetic.
There is denial in these boundaries.

If I was my mother I could unpick
along the lines of this patternstance

but I have no such patience
for knitting or needlework.

The occupancy of a hearthstone oblated.
No less backward than forward

all I forecast is revenue. Am I a wife
doing the impression of a suit or a suit

doing the impression of a wife?
To ask these questions implies failure.

To imply you cannot have it all implies failure.
Cannot stay and also go, cannot love and also fight love.

I want to sleep with other men
so I know I still exist apart and aside from you.

If I objectify myself, if I define boundaries.
A bad way to go about it

but one much practiced
and offering the soft kind of comfort

of morning cups of tea or a baby's stuffed lamb
still kept on the teenage bed.

I want to sleep with Descartes. Certainly in the end
she considers that to be is to be apart.

There is denial in these boundaries
ugly cowardice is rearing its cow-fucked face again.

Too difficult to negotiate with the ego
unwilling to accept the responsibility

for birthing the world again and again,
for its magical transformations.

Remember you capitulate.
The long while since you could tree any argument.

Remember being eighteen and secretly convinced
no matter what happened

you would never, ever forget a single man you slept with.
Then the faces fading into the dark woods of memory

with only the occasional touch
quivering like an arrow into green sap.

How much more beautiful!
To turn, years later, in conversation with an infrequent acquaintance

and recollect suddenly, yes – oh yes!
You can never quite hide the startled expression on your face

how rapidly the realisation has overcome you.
Even behind your glass it is late, and so charmingly clumsy.

There is a grace too to their answering sheepishness.
You eat it candled together.

56. Guilt Is A Fantasy Worth Tending

You light the candle
then you ring the bell to summon her.

You have arranged sliced fruit on a plate
it is fresh and pungent.

You have left out the knife
you wouldn't want her to think

you were deliberately hiding it.
There is some spicy wine too in a fluted glass.

Sit back on your heels and watch the drawn curtains.
Is there a stirring in the thick folds

something deeper than velvet?
There is only the stillness

the steady flare of the candle-flame.
And watch her draw near now

the imagined ghost of your murdered child.
She is always seven or nine

although if living she would be much younger.
She comes and joins you cross-legged

like your inquisitor she is facing you.
She is wearing that pink dress that you always give her.

She puts her head to one side.
You don't do this very often.

Her voice is careful and calm.
It's nothing more than an observation.

No. No, I don't.
Most of the time I don't even think of you.

Are you thinking of me now?
Or of your elaborate preparation?

How staged the scene is.
Would you like him to catch you?

Her voice is still so calm and even.
You have to remember it's yourself that's talking.

So I could hold my pain against him?
Your fictional pain

the ghost is quick to correct.
Yes. So he would have to take care of you.

Isn't that why you construct it.
She sounds almost bored.

She is playing with the candle-flame.
Don't. Please. Stop that.

It's hot. You'll hurt –
Hurt what? The wicked smile, and the laughter.

Your tears never last very long.
Besides, that sickly occult picnic

only really happens in the mind
and so it takes about twenty seconds to occur

and then dissolve again. You're actually aproned
still standing in the kitchen.

He'll be here soon and you need to clear up.
The sink is full, bubbles are piling through your fingers.

You know it's better to use marigolds
but with skin you can know what's really clean or not.

It was all so long ago.
You know if you were back there

you would do exactly the same again.
The greatest crimes are the ones you never regret.

57. Happiness Is An Extension Of The Self

And I can still smell your perfume.
All these thoughts start in the middle

that's the problem.
In the collar-tuck of your coat.

Sucked down like a line
and gone with the same headache rush.

The burning platinum river of the soul
has scoured a living scar.

Call it pain if you can't cope with it.
Call it pain if you can't face it.

Call it pain unless you wrap your hand right round
the fierce white-hot stream

and hold the self
clear and sudden in the centre of the mind.

The light on terracotta chimney pots
brick almost green by comparison.

Safe behind the window
there could be tea here

and a sofa stuffed with happy memories –
Ice-skating, I don't know.

You'll be fine. I'll catch you.
You and that big cheesy grin, huh?

How I smiled and smiled.
Two fires burning at the same height.

Happiness like warm honey.
After skating, going on in the dark

glühwein, bratwurst mit sauerkraut,
pommes frites, churros

rollercoasters and tiny huts
looking like they were made from gingerbread

gathering in the centre for dancing
steins of beer

the feel of his arms around her
when he caught her skating or in the dance.

Three years! Three years
and I still want you beyond imagining.

58. The Traveller Never Escapes The Self

We could move you know.
Get away from London.

New York even.
I could get a transfer.

The New York office is doing worse
than we are.

You know we'd be alright honey.
Pause as his money

washes over her like oil
over a seagull chick.

It wouldn't be different.
We wouldn't be different.

I can't talk when you're like this.
So fucking pessimistic.

The cities of the world
laid out like cocktails.

All of them
will get you fucked.

59. Love Is A Weight We Carry Alone

Like a woman dragging a heavy suitcase
up an icy slope is how I carry my love for you.

Tethered by a brittle plastic handle
of indeterminate but never comfortable length.

The right wheel is slightly adrift and will catch and stick,
sometimes hovering for millennia on a certain pebble

deciding on which side to crash.
You know the ground is uneven beneath its slick coating

and my hands get sore even through gloves.
Shoulders stretched splintering.

Sisyphus' wife, the constant one, never letting go
carrying on up the mobius slope. To let go would be unthinkable

although I often think of it.
Sometimes when the ice is sheer (at its most dangerous)

and my boots slip, the case glissades
weightless – then I feel like I'm flying.

I have broken and sprained several limbs this way
not least some mild finger-bones of that fist in the chest

that circus squeezebox.
You do not have to notice how 'finger-bones'

has exactly the same syllables
and emphasis as 'ventricles'.

Less metaphorically, there's a sneaking suspicion
of permanent damage to the whole limbic system

another vague animal. For some ancient religions
the liver was the seat of the soul.

But it is hard to find a doctor in the dark night
and even if I could stop

how could I leave this case out
in the cold and snow? There is a bite of snow coming in the air

crisp like an apple taken newly from the tree.
For surely there would be no room for it

in his little apothecary's shop
with its potions and instruments

its long shelves of stacked jars,
the musty herbs crowding from the ceiling

hung by the black chanticleer? How wildly
the glass eye glares from beneath that clotted comb.

And here he comes like a gaunt bird himself
nosecone stuffed with rosemary.

His hands are arthritic and slow.
He indicates the open door of the iron maiden.

Stepping gingerly past the eye of newt
and anatomical skeleton

on the wall an elderly portrayal of Galen's pig
watches mournfully. The men in togas are cheering

as the knife pierces the last vertebrae
and its legs collapse and the door slowly clangs shut...

I wake on the slope, as I always wake
with crushed blood and ice in my mouth.

I have fallen again. Chipped a tooth and bloodied lip
though I've not the time now for that examination.

My mind blanks in sudden panic
but my right hand is still frozen around the handle of the case

in irretrievable marriage.
I struggle to my feet and continue on.

60. In A Capitalist World We Must Own Our Own Bodies

Like everything in life it is to be faced alone.
I was solitary

at my childhood's murder and
solitary at my own child's murder.

Really it was so it could be secret
from him, so he didn't go running.

Too early. The child was a playing card
I stacked the deck.

Guilt in storage like jam
packed up for winter months.

You can't own him
otherwise people would own you.

Entering the ring from the side of desire:
you are guilty because you want children.

Entering from the poets' corner
long trail of blood behind the suitcase:

My love is my child.
My fear of love is my child.

It's a moot point. Juliette's face reflected back
in the window in the moonlight. The child is dead.

61. Schrödinger's Problem

There could be another child
would it stop him from leaving me?

Dirty little thoughts at 4am
still wrapped in his spunky linen.

Cat in a box
cat in a box

dead or alive
you're a cat in a box.

The hyperactive mind latching on
to any literary, scientific or social props

that describe with the greatest melodrama
the state of indecision.

Do I ask him if he slept with her or not?
The cat

only remembers being alive.
Juliette only remembers being married.

62. Selling Is Authentic Because Our Natures Are Transactional

'There's no such thing as a bad customer
only a bad salesperson.' Waking

in the middle of the night
drenched in sweat at the thought of it.

At the constant responsibility
to remake the world.

Remake yourself for them
until you make the sale.

But for what sort of person is an authentic act
an act of sale?

Blood has no statute.
Marie failed to hit her target.

Good salespeople can sell anything
because what they're selling is themselves.

No coincidence Christian morality
is at the forefront of capitalism.

If you cannot fracture in these ceaseless transactions…
Snap back, smell the coffee.

Your good money for my product.
Your bomb for my burnt-out building

your terrorist architecture
for a wasteland of mauve.

Now redevelopment, the inscription:
upgraded societal space.

I have consulted with the architect
but can find nowhere in the plans an escape hatch

or similar contingency in case of fire
or if you should want to leave the building abruptly and secretively

following such incidents as getting caught on your knees
with the boss's cock in your mouth

or simply because of that particular shade of taupe on the walls.
Put frankly you can't make a break for it.

A break is synonymous with a rupture
hence will cause a remaking.

Here in the building you are forever
taking part in transactions.

You might as well be authentic about it.
I will speak again with the architect.

I think I can convince him to add a swimming pool
big enough to hold all of your tears.

63. Does Adultery Harm A Marriage If By Definition It Takes Place Outside It

Honeymoon mornings stretch
like endless school playing fields.

Not to kiss would be to wound.
That is why there is Spanish guitar music.

Contentment brags the door open to boredom
like one small citrused Hoegaarden

on a summer afternoon
can bring you to your gutter knees

DJ-spun at 4am.
Who should she blame most?

Memory, its theatre of blind alleys.
That one brief infidelity

was maybe his way of affirming his vows.
Is my husband a lying cheating bastard

and my best friend an amoral slut?
That's better don't dress it up.

Dress it up and it loses the impact
that has stopped her heart in its thick bone carriage

for three days.
The sleek white coupe of her own guiltlessness

is risking a submersion in dogshit.
For she has been the other woman herself of course.

Darling we have been betrayed by passion
bound and bedraggled by our senseless sex.

Through this opening we can look out
onto the wide green sea of not-being-together.

Because the door is open and I can see freedom.
Because the cage is unlocked.

Darling if I leave you
it is because you didn't make me stay.

You didn't call the police
send speeding cars to follow me.

How did this all get so out of control?
All I ever wanted was for us to be drunk and never unhappy.

To eat toasted cheese sandwiches in bed together.
But you're too classy for that shit.

64. Money Is The Value Of Desire

Stand up to be counted
you stand up to be shot.

The government will bail the banks out
anyway.

The most valuable thing to do
is keep spending.

We have mojitos to drink.
We have a skiing holiday in February.

These are the good lives.
This is what we paid for.

Money is good.
You can buy happiness.

We have no needs.
We exist purely in a state of desire.

65. Art Should Acknowledge The Privilege Of The Narrative

So hard to talk to people
when you are used to being inside them.

The narrator of the story
the screen actor alone in his room.

Then the creation of avatars seems natural.
Spielberg the shit out of it.

But consumption is empty
without reaction.

At least we have music.
Here you are again with your small thunders

chords like prehistoric claws
against the brontide of the bass.

Many-mythed, with your triple bolt
of verse, chorus, bridge.

The heaviest drum sounding
like a whale dropping back into the sea.

Old Tarhunt sits at the bar
offering up his eyes and heart.

He'll betray you, son, you and your bird both.
Don't sink to his alcoholic melancholy

don't sleep on any floors you might stick to.
Wield your wood like a totem

pull back on your feathers and beak.
By midnight you can blink sheet lightening

the strobe encircling you like a glowing snake.
You are cutting temples for the nubile whores to sport in

in their ripped bleach jeans and scaly sequin skins.
There's something about a man with an axe

which chops them off at the knees
their little red caps fluttering in submission.

Illuyanka thinks she's been chosen
twists her hips with that rippling effect.

There's a delay between your fingers and the riff splitting
so she can count how close you are.

Will the sea of creatures at your feet pull you in?
There's something elemental going on here

a tension between two types of wave.
At the last note, for one final nanosecond

before another sort of thunder
we can see shuddering behind your bowed head

some kind of mirage or shattered vision
a mountain hovering in the air.

66. Money Is An Invisible Comfort Until

You remember your mistakes more than your triumphs
because you learn from them.

From triumphs you learn little.
But sometime what you remember

will be walking across the stone tiles
in the house by Pezenas

each step felt like it was being imprinted
in freshly made bread.

Sometimes you will remember the rough grain
of the unfinished doorframe.

There is a joy
which is not subject to triumph.

A longer learning and harder joy
like the stone at the centre of the sweet peach.

The sudden growl of the espresso machine wakes you.
You drive to see the bulls in a fast Ferrari

it is a red cape to the wind.
Crowds are already cheering

the empty orange sand.
That continuum of arches

is you arriving again and again.
Tenderbreak.

Heart into dust
then dough again.

Love at last
the white oleander

counting cicadas on the path
with their little red bums.

The open earth where
the elephantine stumps plug in.

Love, dust, schist permitting
the black grape.

The blood of the toro
vino, a golden arm in sunlight.

67. Who Cares If They Love Us

To arrive without memory
like stone, like metal.

Like sunlight, like graffiti.
I'm not afraid to die

I'm afraid of losing my job.
We don't care if our lovers love us

we care if our clients love us.
I don't want to vote for a government

I want to go out every Friday night
and drink cocktails and take cocaine

and take pills and take photos
and post them on Facebook.

I'm afraid of weighing more than nine stone.
I'm afraid I'll never get pregnant.

It's not important that you cheated
it's important that I found out.

Keep their mouths shut they can have you
it won't diminish my experience of you.

Who is the enemy. That's what young people
in my country can't understand.

Time like a language
writing across consciousness.

This is not a war. We are all getting out of this
alive. Whether you want to or not.

68. Super Marriage = Not Transcending Each Other

Where's that man of yours tonight?
Working late. Some last minute deal.

What does he do again?
Something that keeps me in French perfume.

Gales of laughter
shake all the tension from your body

like you can only do with true friends.
This might not be an irrevocable act.

People lose their jobs all the time.
Marie might come back.

Juliette isn't listening.
She wants to get beyond marriage

through marriage and out the other side.
She wants to be super-married

above marriage, a space
where they will not transcend one another.

There has to be a third exit
not the beforehand of not-being-married

or the afterwards of death or divorce
sewn together by an infinitely rupturing present

How do I circle above the process
like a hawk circling prey?

69. When We Are Afraid We Tear Others Down

The first day away from you
is always bliss.

The second finds me steamingly
unhappy, millet-mouthed and shivery.

Yes, the second day is like coming
to the shingled end of the beach.

The toast is stale, the butter is sour
the coffee is weak.

Where is the dreaming sharp mind of yesterday
the self being a fortress?

Now its walls are overgrown with moss and lichen
the battlements crumble

chunks of discarded masonry fill the moat
amongst the trash of tourist soft drink bottles

cigarette packets and paper tissues.
The cigarettes reassert some latent energy.

You are not the crowd with their sun block
and rolls of fat.

You are in the little tabac stall by the drawbridge
smoking endless Gauloises

with Jean-Paul Belmondo.
It has made the coffee taste better.

70. To Be A Wife Is To Depend

Arguments. Arguments
you neve dreamed you could have.

But we always go to Val D'Isere.
I want to try something different.

I'll pay for it.
You'll pay? Oh come on honey.

You're my wife.
You're not supposed to be independent.

Lord give me the strength
to live through conflict

through not being one thing
or the other.

71. Only The People We Love Can Hurt Us Deeply

To cease the pain, you must cease the value
that you give to the love-object.

Counterpoint: If you love someone so much
doesn't any amount of pain become bearable?

The pain becomes part of the value.
She wonders

if it would be the same if he hit her
if the abuse was physical.

She thinks she might prefer it.
She knows that this is melodrama.

You're not picking up when I call you.
My phone battery dies like everyone else's.

The pain of not knowing builds a solid carapace
around her love. Holding it steady.

72. To Be Known Is To Be Weak

Something has put its hands around the throat of the future
and is constricting it.

Deliciously deciding the shape our life will take
all this is now forbidden.

As if I had walked into the nursery
and found the child stillborn.

To be known is to be weak.
The familiar can be discarded.

All the novels are wrong.
When I am alone and give way to grief

this is what I am chanting.
All the novels are wrong.

When I cry I rock backward and forward.
Another attractive trait.

I need to demand attention
the way a poem demands attention

like a beautiful woman dancing
in the centre of the room.

She is very young, the girl at the bar
in her long black cardigan.

He is laughing with her.
When was the last time you laughed together?

A cobwebbed memory. Still you carry it bound in amber
on a gold chain around your neck.

Maybe we should move to the country.
Maybe we should get a dog

with fur the colour of ripe wheat.
The wheat ripe at the bottom of the garden

Everything could be fecund and fresh.
When was the last time we went out together?

73. Little Robot Of Deceit

Little robot of deceit
little ferryman of desire.

Silver as a fish and more difficult to capture.
All slimmed out and palm-slick.

It is mental how much you record.
Your speed is mental.

We have to burn letters.
But you. You yield to a thumb.

You are immediate in your dichotomies
both archivist and whisper.

Little instrument, little flute of should-not-be-told.
And so clinical in your usefulness, your variant capacity.

I can take you to the movies but you must not spit
like violinists at a bus stop.

If you were more real you would not pass so smoothly
your lead weight on the rubber sheet of those scribbles and tongue.

Your power is not yours but you will hold it.
More holder than held, your tiny church of truth.

But never the whole truth.
Little shuffler of the deck of thoughts

little vision of the Other.
Bigger gods than you have shattered fewer worlds.

74. The Tiger God Husband

For what could you imagine
that love would fade.

Of course he doesn't hit her.
It's just occasionally he has hit her.

As long as you keep making decisions
it will all be fine.

Decision like, I deserve to be hit
if I hit him first.

Decision like, I will ignore he is fucking my best friend
until he admits it.

When love fades the sex is terrible
sex that was always so handcuffs and whipped cream.

Going to the theatre not wearing panties
his hand slips up her leg in the taxi.

When does it suddenly become clear
clear like a summer rain that there is

will be no love of your life?
That you are Barbie mything up outdated social stereotypes.

All this mess needs to be cleared out of the way.
All this pride in the false subjugation of your Tiger God Husband.

(Let me explain to you about the Tiger God Husband.
This is not your husband. This is not anyone's husband.

Even goddesses do not have a husband
like the Tiger God Husband.

The Tiger God Husband is made of woman parts
part of skin and teeth and bone and mostly wishing.

Part of him is the moon
and you know what happens when you wish for that.

Part of him is a tiger skin
 even though that's illegal and immoral.

And you were the one who built this
so feel bad about it and rightly so.

The Tiger God Husband does not speak
he only smiles his tiger teeth.

All carved out of you like a rib out of Adam.
He is a talisman who has slept under your pillow

since you were five. He keeps eating souls
because you keep feeding them to him.

Only the best souls for the Tiger God Husband.
In fact we all know it's your soul.

But you like to pretend you're in a mirror like Alice
and he is really consuming the souls of those other men

too pale and indistinct to be husbands.
What he is doing is tipping the balance.

What he is doing to making impossible promises
one could only wish to keep.

Keep your Tiger God Husband in your toybox
do not let him out. If you let him out you will marry.

You will be unhappy because your husband
is not a Tiger God.

You will try to pretend he is a Tiger God
but god knows, he is not.

The Tiger God Husband does not exist.
For this reason you can stay married to him forever

and maybe this is the best option.
Do not go around foisting your myths on other people.)

The problem is if he is not a Tiger God
you are not really sure you can love him.

You keep running into these other people with Tiger God masks
and quivering suddenly like a naked dove.

75. She Wants Him To Be In Love. He Wants A Wife

It's true that if we hadn't been drunk
we wouldn't have fought.

When she moves forward
it is like a knight on a chessboard.

She only gets a little way
before she veers off on a tangent.

She understands if they can't get drunk together
the relationship is over.

I want to fix this thing that makes us fight.
These insecurities I have.

He gets drunk too.
Why do I have to be the one who controls myself?

The discourse is breaking up.
She wants to say, we're supposed to be in love.

76. Sacrifice Time To Make Yourself Beautiful

At the beginning they say call me
text me whenever you want

I just want to hear your sexy voice.
While they're still in the hunt.

After a few months
Why are you texting me in the middle of the day?

I'm at work, babe.
Why are you texting on a Friday night?

I'm out with my friends.
Don't you have friends of your own?

You can't follow me all the time.
These little boys never heard the story

of Snow White, Cinderella, Sleeping Beauty.
Only girls get taught that.

Fuck you he says
Why don't you take care of yourself like other girls?

Don't call him. Don't message him.
Go to the salon, get your nails done.

Even if you are slobbing in your pjs
make sure they are silk.

They compare you to posters.
They compare you to their friends' girlfriends.

For the man-boys, the Peter Pans
the natural state of a woman is mascara and jewellery.

They do not want your passion.
They want you bent over in a nurse's uniform.

Your success in your job
is due to the advice I gave you.

You're not happy
because you don't behave like I tell you.

All I ever wanted was you to be here.
This is what she put on the plate to be eaten

by someone who doesn't understand hunger.
What he offered... she can't remember.

She offered herself the dream of love
and it was his job to kiss her, to wake her up.

To end the dream. She finally has it.
His job was to end love.

77. Atrocities

War is an atrocity committed by men.
Love is an atrocity committed by women.

Gender is an atrocity committed by society.
For the person who loves

trying to see the other's not-love
is like trying to hear darkness, see silence.

78. Intellectuals' Function Is To Appreciate Art

Can you feel a thing
if you don't have a word for it?

She tastes her own name... Juliette.
Something sticks in her teeth.

Why do you have to turn everything
into a competition?

How much he earns.
How many fucking books you've read.

These days every time she thinks of him
she thinks of burning paper.

She cannot make out
if they are bills or pages.

79. Memory Is Not Your Friend

Memory arrives and catches her off-guard.
Memory of the swimming pool at night

his hands on her waist
the perfect heat.

Wet bodies sliding together.
And later in the bath

she took him in her mouth.
How to throw all this away?

Men can separate desire of the body
from desire of the person.

80. By Expressing Our Desire We Make Ourselves Weak

Boldly I told you I wanted you
said I wanted to fuck you yes.

What did my boldness get me?
The memory of love. Not love itself.

If I had been meek.
If I had been another girl – but no

always one drink too many
always one remark too feminist

always one doctrine too intellectual.
Always some reference to Plato

which remarks me as iron not silk.
Who would sleep with a crowbar.

Who would sleep with a nail.
Silk tears beautifully. Iron rusts.

As a child I would chew on my mother's old bra springs.
Tasted like blood.

I am sure it was not like this in the beginning.
I am sure I had some sense of self.

Yet I have turned myself into
a reflection of desire.

81. Lying Silver Tongue

Three thousand pounds the sofa.
Five thousand pounds the bed.

Oh god the underfloor heating.
The silk curtains handmade. The vintage chandeliers.

The gold card is having an orgasm
plastic genie, superchipped

wired and transmitting at each transaction
glorying in the blows, the casual violence of wealth.

If it could speak I. I like the chaise longue
but darling, that coffee table has to go!

Rectify. Reswipe. Love the firm click of insertion.
Love the heroin rush of being online.

Plug me in baby! And above all, to be used.
Five star hotel in Morocco. Cartier watch.

Never ask me how rich you are
I will spit and splutter like an angry parrot.

I am your slim tool of consumption
I am not here to provide you information.

I can give you back only your own name, embossed.
Run your thumb along it, pretend you know braille.

Buy another useless trinket for the stainless steel kitchen
you use max once a week.

If you want staff I can pay for them.
Why should you scrub your own floor

just because your mother does
and her mother did before her?

Let me take you away from all of this.
Let's take him for all he's worth.

The sick feeling rises suddenly in her mouth.
Goes to her handbag takes it out gets the scissors.

Can she. She can't. She yes she can yes she cuts it up.
Right through the lying silver tongue.

Sighs. Picks up the phone to call the bank
and order a new one.

82. Desire Cannot Sustain Respect

We bulldoze over all good advice.
He's very manly, I suppose.

She revels in his masculinity.
If only they had never been happy

if only it had all been a game.
But reality's too cruel to permit that.

She shivers as she steps out of her jogging shorts.
Now the dress it's important

it is the frame through which he sees her.
The mint or the peach?

Feels so 1950s.
Like a doll in the mirror.

She sits. She sits down.
She sits down thinks oh my god what is this.

Jewellery that I can't afford
a marriage that I can't respect.

Where the only thing between us is sex.
Great hooks ripping into her sides.

No wonder he slept with Marie.
He's bored. I'm bored.

Anger hovers above her on a string
she is pulling it down

it is coming down and engulfing her.
No! Not my destruction.

She gets. She gets up.
She gets up she puts on her white sandals.

She gets up she takes her handbag.
Leaves the credit card riven on the countertop.

She gets up she puts on her sandals
she takes her handbag she walks.

She walks down the stairs to the front door she opens it.
Do not look back. Don't. She walks.

She walks down the stairs to the front door
she opens it she leaves

She leaves she goes out of the gate into the street
the street with its sunshine and magnolia.

Parked cars. People walking past
they don't know what she's doing

the enormity the fracture across the horizon the end of the world
the end of love the casting aside of desire.

She walks she leaves she goes out onto the street
into the sunshine she leaves she flies

she is like aeroplanes knife-bright blades in the sky.
She is the dove the warm feathers stretching and rising.

There is only her.
There was always only her.

Thanks & Acknowledgements

These poems have never been published before anywhere. However, some extended prose pieces from which certain of them were drawn saw the light of day in *The Prague Revue* (now defunct).

This book was written sporadically over many years and as I moved about different locales. Three women in particular sustained my poetic practice throughout those years: in Prague, Sarah Borufka; in Paris, Kate Noakes; and in Dubai, Zeina Hashem Beck. My gratitude knows no bounds. Thanks are due to Salena Godden and Tim Wells, for never losing touch. Tim Wells and Alec Newman helped edit some of these poems when they first found form. Thanks also to Janette Ayachi for the enthusiastic welcome when I rocked up in Edinburgh. Further back, a Jerwood/Arvon Young Poets' Apprenticeship in 2003 was the first recognition I had of being a 'real' poet. Thanks to Jackie Kay for putting me up for it and Carol Rumens for her mentorship. A brief membership of Roddy Lumsden's City University group when I lived in London taught me an enormous amount in a short time. He trusted something in me before I did.

Thanks to Rob for being an amazing editor, and to my mum and dad for raising me to be above all open-minded. And finally, to Ed, who proved to me that not all relationships have to be as toxic as Juliette's.

Annie Brechin received a Jerwood/Arvon Young Poets Apprenticeship in 2003 at the age of 19. After stints living, writing and performing in Prague, Paris and Dubai, she has settled down in Edinburgh. *The Mouth of Eulalie* is her first full-length collection.